HOW TO MAKE YOUR MARRIAGE LAST

A Wife's Guide

ANN BENTON

Commendations

In this little gem Ann helpfully unpacks the Bible's recipe for a delicious marriage and then seasons it with her own insight and godly wisdom.

Kath Paterson, wife of Andy Paterson, Mission Director of FIEC

Vintage Ann—straight-talking, biblical and wise! Full of practical advice, this is a must-read for every wife who wants to protect her marriage.

Daphne Ross, pastor's wife, Farnham Baptist Church

This booklet is so brief you can read it in a single sitting, yet so full of biblical truths, clearly taught, illustrated and applied, that you'll want to return to it again and again. Ann unpacks gender difference and submission in Christian marriage in a way that makes you want to give it a go and reap the rewards of a marriage that lasts.

Carolyn Bickersteth, rector's wife, Arborfield and Barkham Churches, Reading

© Day One Publications 2015

First printed 2015

ISBN 978-1-84625-480-2

British Library Cataloguing in Publication Data available

Published by Day One Publications, Ryelands Road, Leominster, HR6 8NZ

Telephone 01568 613 740 FAX 01568 611 473

email—sales@dayone.co.uk

web site—www.dayone.co.uk

Cover design by Rob Jones, Elk Design

Printed by Orchard Press Cheltenham

Contents

You have to do more than just want a lasting marriage, and certainly more than merely expect it.

Introduction: Always

I'll be loving you always,
With a love that's true, always
When the things you've planned
Need a helping hand
I will understand always
Always
Days may not be fair always
That's when I'll be there, always
Not for just an hour
Not for just a day
Not for just a year
But always

Thus goes Irving Berlin's romantic song, which could appropriately be sung at a wedding by the ones who make their vows. It is a song of commitment— for richer, for poorer, for better, for worse, and all that. But according to 2012 data from the Office for National Statistics, 42 per cent of marriages in England and Wales end in divorce. Marriages are apparently most at risk during the first ten years, and the chance of divorce is greatest between the fourth and eighth wedding anniversaries.

So sentiments and promises sincerely expressed on a wedding day do not in themselves guarantee a lasting marriage. Nor does a Christian faith, as too many of us are aware and must acknowledge with sorrow and shame. The old picture of a Christian marriage as a triangle, with the Lord himself as the third corner (the closer each party is to Christ, the closer each is to the other), makes some kind of point, but it belies the fact that a union between two ransomed sinners requires a good deal of sustained effort to mitigate the corroding effects of sin.

You have to do more than just *want* a lasting marriage, and certainly more than merely expect it. Novelist George Eliot, a perceptive observer of human relationships, wrote this in her novel *Daniel Deronda* (first published in 1876) on the subject of marriage:

> In general mortals have a great power of being astonished at the presence of an effect towards which they have done everything, and at the absence of an effect towards which they have done nothing but desire it ... Husbands and wives are mutually astonished at the loss of an affection which they have taken no pains to keep.

If that was true in Victorian times when divorce was a big no-no in respectable society, how much more so in the me-first twenty-first century when divorce is almost the new normal! Perhaps we should be surprised, and grateful, at the number of marriages which do stand the test of time.

And yet God designed marriage to last (Matthew 19:6). 'Always' is a God-type word. To break faith with each other in marriage is analogous to God breaking faith with his people—unthinkable!

Having been in pastoral life for thirty-five years, I have listened and talked to a large number of women as they have discussed their marriages. It tends to be women who are the ones who read books on marriage and women who are the first to open up about problems in their marriages. My husband, John, and I have generally maintained that to save a failing or struggling marriage, both parties should be willing participants in any discussions. But what if a husband is unwilling to admit there is any deficiency? A man who is unwilling to ask a stranger for directions when he is lost is going to be even less willing to ask a pastor for help in a marriage that is going off the rails. What does a wife do then?

Of course she can pray. And that is what she must do first and continually. A number of recent publications have drawn attention to the power of a praying wife. But the first letter of Peter has some other pointers. Writing to God's chosen people suffering a range of difficulties in life, not least persecution, he urged them to remember that they should regard themselves as 'aliens and strangers' in this world and live the kind of life among the pagans that would bring glory to God (1 Peter 2:9–12). Peter then goes on to illustrate and apply this in a range of scenarios, and in chapter 3 he comes to marriage, with some words for wives. He pictures a believing woman married to a difficult man. Perhaps, but not necessarily, the husband is an unbeliever (1 Peter 3:1–2). Peter's argument is that winsomeness, not words, will win the day. She can be proactive in glorifying God in her marriage even when her husband is not signing up for a marriage refresher course.

The key word here is 'submission'. To modern ears this is a horrendous word, redolent of jackboots, concentration camps and doormats. But read on, reader, read on—more on this later in the booklet. The encouragement for any woman is that she can do something to improve her marriage and make it last. She can attend to her own heart, which will make her more beautiful and permeate her behaviour.

> Your beauty should not come from outward adornment, such as braided hair and the wearing of gold jewellery and fine clothes. Instead, it should be that of your inner self, the unfading beauty of a gentle and quiet spirit, which is of great worth in God's sight (1 Peter 3:3–4).

So here are some thoughts offered to women who from their side want not merely to maintain but to nourish and strengthen their marriages; who want to love, not just for a year, but always.

Men and women, equally
made by God, equally given
what is known as the creation
mandate (Genesis 1:28) to be
fruitful and multiply and
to rule over the earth, are
different by design and for a
reason.

1. Understand the implications of the essential differences

Marriage is a covenant between a man and a woman (Genesis 2:24; Matthew 19:4–5)—the Bible recognizes no other definition—and male and female are two different things. Men and women are different by design. So I say to all female readers of this booklet: you must realize that you are promising to love and cherish an alien species. He is not the same as you; God has brought him to you to be your head and your protector, the father of your children and your partner in service. And in order for him to do that and be that, God has given him a different make-up from yours.

Many books have been written about gender distinctives, and even the ultimate arch-feminist acknowledges that these differences exist. We say things like 'It's a chick-flick' or 'It's a man thing', and we all understand what we mean.

Some people see the differences as merely cultural, a matter of programming and training. But studies again and again show that they are not. Of course there are cultural distinctions. Where I live, men do not wear dresses, for example, but there are plenty of places in the world where they do. That is a cultural distinction and it is perfectly benign. Girls using a female public toilet is a benign cultural distinction. No one is picketing the public toilets and shouting about discrimination.

Some cultural distinctions are less benign; for example, the one that says that only boys can have an education and that girls must stay at home and learn to cook and keep house. Such distinctions are wrong and unhelpful, and find no support in the Bible.

Yet there are differences which are based on absolutes. Genesis 1:27 tells us that God made humans in two kinds, male and female. Men and women, equally made by God, equally given what is known as the creation mandate (Genesis 1:28) to be fruitful and multiply and to rule over the earth, are different by design and for a reason. Even thinking very broadly and biologically, you know this is true. Men are generally stronger in the upper body than women; a woman's strongest muscles are in her uterus. Doesn't that tell you something about design and purpose? God deliberately made two genders. There are also numerous physiological and neurological differences which show that men and women think in different ways—not entirely differently, but still in significantly different ways.

It is beyond the remit of this booklet to explore the gender issue in more depth. If these ideas are strange or confusing to you, I refer you to *Recovering Biblical Manhood and Womanhood* by John Piper and Wayne Grudem,[1] or, for a shorter read, *Gender Questions* by John Benton.[2] The point here is that men and women are equal but different. They complement each other.

We are different by design and for a purpose. And one place where that difference will be seen is in your marriage—not in the question of who does the housework, but predominantly in the question of how you relate to each other.

Why do we expect men to be the same as us? When we do so we are likely to meet frustration and marital disharmony. We are not meant to duplicate each other but to complement each other. Studies of male and female brains indicate that in the male brain, the left and right brains function independently, whereas in the female brain, left and right and the bits in between are totally engaged in any thinking; there are lights going on all over the place. Forgive my non-scientific descriptions: I realize I am explaining it rather crudely and broadly. Nevertheless, the following two distinctions are ones you will probably recognize, and I have found it helpful in my own marriage to bear them in mind.

Tunnel vision
God made the man to be work-focused. He created Adam out of the dust of the ground to work the ground, whereas Eve was created out of Adam's rib and she is always more interested in people and relationships. Meanwhile, he wants to get on with the job. When a man takes on something, he is totally into it: he intends to get to the end of it and achieve.

Interestingly, male peripheral vision is generally less good than that of the female. She has the wide-angle lens, taking in the whole picture; he is sticking to the point. A woman's mind can be on several things at once, quite truly. She is the one who wakes up on a Saturday morning with a list and makes her husband afraid.

Male hearing is similarly focused. He really doesn't hear you when he is listening to the Test Match, whereas you can listen to the radio and have a conversation simultaneously.

My husband and I have frequently enjoyed visiting museums together, but he is focused on his route and the particular things he wants to see, and then the exit. He enjoys it, but it is a task to be done. Meanwhile, I get distracted and wander. When we go shopping together he wants to know precisely what I am looking for, and he gets confused and exasperated when I divert because I have a whim to look at cookers, watches or lampshades.

Again, forgive the generalization—of course there is a spectrum in this—but the man is made to want to get to the bottom line, the result. That is what will make him effective in his work. For him, life is compartmentalized, and a specialized approach makes sense and works.

Recognize, understand, appreciate and love it.

The performance mindset

God has made the man to provide and protect. The model here is Christ himself, who is described as feeding and caring for the church (Ephesians 5:29). The Lord himself taught us to pray, 'Give us today our daily bread' (Matthew 6:11). So it is part of biblical manhood to take on the mantle of protector and provider in an active way.

I know many talkative men. But as a rule, the male sex prefers doing to talking, and their talk is more in their heads. They are more interested in achievement and performance than in attitude and feelings.

The implication of this for me as a wife is that when John does not talk, it does not mean there is something wrong. On the other hand, when I don't talk, John is perfectly correct in deducing that there is something wrong (usually I witter away).

This recognition also explains to me my husband's extraordinary level of frustration when we meet traffic congestion on a journey. Unless we have a binding deadline to meet, an extended car journey is not for me the huge downer it is for him. Why? Because I am happy (normally) to think that it is just more time to have my husband to myself and enjoy his company, his conversational input on my burning issues or some music together. But his preoccupation is with getting there. Even at its most scintillating, the pleasure of my repartee is ranked well below the pleasure of objective achieved. Journey's end means job done.

The performance mindset means that a man needs to feel capable of solving his own and your problems. This is why, when you share with him a disappointment or challenge, he immediately offers solutions. But sometimes all you wanted was sympathy, not solutions. Understand his mindset. He is just being a man. Solutions is what he does.

This is also why it will usually be the wife who will suggest asking someone for directions when you are lost in a strange town. He doesn't like doing it because it makes him feel a failure that he couldn't solve this one himself.

And most importantly, the performance mindset is the reason why your husband might be over-sensitized to feeling nagged when all you were doing was mentioning something. Your talk, your thinking out loud, your Saturday morning list sounds like asking for a solution. And action—now.

Understand the implications of the essential differences.

Notes

1   John Piper and Wayne Grudem, eds., *Recovering Biblical Manhood and Womanhood: A Response to Evangelical Feminism* (Wheaton, IL: Crossway, 2006).

2   John Benton, *Gender Questions: Biblical Manhood and Womanhood in the Contemporary World* (Darlington: Evangelical Press, 2000).

God has designed you to be
the protected one, while your
husband does the protecting.

2. Get it straight about submission

It is impossible to do a Bible study on wifehood without coming fairly quickly to the word or concept of 'submission'. The classic wedding Scripture reading of Ephesians 5:22–33, the training older women are supposed to give younger wives in the local church (Titus 2:5) and the words Peter has for believing women in a non-ideal marriage in 1 Peter 3 all include it. It is not the only aspect of a woman's relationship with her husband: elsewhere in Scripture she is referred to as her husband's partner (Malachi 2:14) and as his helper (Genesis 2:18). She is to love her husband (Titus 2:4), and yet as we have seen from that same paragraph in Titus, still be subject to him.

This is the way marriage—which, remember, is God's invention—is supposed to work and works best. God has defined its shape, and the shape is that the husband is the head and the wife's response to that headship is submission. That is the recipe for the best that the marriage institution can offer. Why try to rewrite the rules?

But before I am drowned out in a social media clamour or an avalanche of hate mail, let me say some things about what submission is not.

Submission does not mean that a woman has no voice

Don't go and crawl into a hole. Your role is to be your husband's helper and lover. How can you do that if you crawl into a hole? You have work to do. As we have seen, God gave the creation mandate to rule over creation to both male and female.

Not only so, but within your marriage your servant-leader will want to know your desires so that he will have the opportunity to feel accomplished about how happy he makes you. Remember the performance mindset.

More importantly, a Christian husband's model for headship is the Lord Jesus Christ himself, whose aim is to make his church, aka his bride, radiant. How can she blossom and flourish if she is downtrodden?

So to express your desires, hopes and dreams is a good thing to do. And in a marriage between sinners you have to learn to say 'ouch' so that he knows what to avoid. Your husband does not want to hurt you; it's just that he's not a mind reader. Sometimes you have to gently tell him.

A wise husband learns to value his wife's voice. She brings unique and precious insight and intuition to any discussion because of the radar equipment which God has installed her with. This is all part of her being a helper.

Proverbs 31 describes a God-fearing woman who throughout her life uses her many gifts and talents for the good of her family and the wider community. She multitasks for Israel. And her husband has full confidence in her and lacks nothing of value (v. 11). She is not stifled, and yet it is clear that her husband who is respected at the city gate (v. 23) is the head of that family. He is stronger and wiser and richer for this wife of noble character, and he knows it.

> Many women do noble things,
>> but you surpass them all (Proverbs 31:29).

Far from being stifled, she has brought her skills and strengths to her marriage and home, and enriched them both.

Submission does not mean that you are inferior

Husband and wife equally bear God's image. The Bible says that you are heirs together (1 Peter 3:7). He is not bound for a bigger share of glory than you. It is true that in one sense you are the weaker vessel: you are probably physically more fragile than your husband. You are the Ming vase; he is the iron pot. Is that a bad thing? God has designed you to be the protected one, while your husband does the protecting. What's not to like about that? It certainly doesn't make you inferior if you are the one for whom someone stronger takes the hard knocks for love of you.

Think of Lizzie Bennett and Mr Darcy in Jane Austen's *Pride and Prejudice*. My favourite scene of the matchless 1995 BBC adaptation was not the famous one where Mr D dives into the lake at Pemberley and emerges with that dripping wet shirt. No, the best scene—and one which set every female heart in Britain a-fluttering—was the one near the end when Darcy proposes for the second time. Lizzie haltingly tries to express her gratitude on behalf of her family for the time and expense Darcy had proffered in order to sort out the Lydia/Wickham scandal. And what does Darcy say? Something like this: 'Much as I respect your family, I believe I thought only of you.' Oh boy, is that romantic! Do you see what is going on there? Sacrificial love. Servant leadership. Was Lizzie offended? Not one whit. Did she feel inferior? No way. She knew she was loved. Give me the unreconstructed male every time. It is the pattern of Christ, the one who loved the church and *gave himself* for her. That is in one sense a measure of her worth as well as of his immense love.

That's the deal. And I and many other women in their right senses would settle for it.

Submission does not mean that you must allow abuse
Colossians 3:18 says, 'Wives, submit to your husbands, as is fitting in the Lord.' This puts a limit on the wife's submission, as does the general principle from Acts 5:29 about obeying God rather than men.

It is most certainly not fitting that in the name of submission you actively or passively aid or abet your husband in behaviour which is wrong. Cruelty and physical abuse is wrong. It would be quite right to blow the whistle on anything of that kind, whether experienced by yourself as a wife or by your children. Talk about it to someone—a pastor, elder or trusted friend. Act similarly if your husband has an addiction or is chronically unfaithful.

You are not there to empower wrong behaviour.

Submission does not mean that a woman must submit to every man on the planet
We are all called upon to submit to God (James 4:7). We are all called upon to submit to civil authorities (Romans 13:5). But submission of a woman to her husband in marriage is personal and specific to that relationship. And that is because of what human marriage represents. It is pre-eminently designed as a visual aid of the love and commitment of Christ to his people.

Many people have been pleased to point out that Ephesians 5:22 ('Wives, submit to your husbands as to the Lord') is preceded by Ephesians 5:21:

> Submit to one another out of reverence for Christ.

Aha, they say, it is a mutual submission! We all submit to each other! Now, apart from the fact that that is faintly ridiculous and presents an image of a bunch of Christians standing by an open door and all saying, 'After you, Claude,' it is not what this part of the apostle's teaching is about.

Of course Christians should be considerate of each other, and there are plenty of other places in the New Testament which say that. But the context here is different. After a load of teaching about church relationships and conduct, Paul is now turning his attention to particular settings for Christian behaviour. He specifies three, namely, marriage (husbands/wives), the workplace (slaves/masters) and the family (parents/children). All of these are situations where there is a God-given authority structure. The teaching is about how to behave when you are in one of these situations. Each of these three settings calls for submission or obedience by one of the parties, though not by the other. They are authority/submission situations. And Paul is saying at this point in his letter: when you are in an authority/submission setting, you submit out of reverence for Christ.

In other words, submission, when it is called for, is something you do for Jesus.

The situations are the very reverse of mutual submission. Wives are to submit to their husbands, not husbands their wives; slaves are to obey their masters, not masters their slaves; children are to obey their parents, not parents their children. Indeed, perhaps precisely because an authority/submission situation might be one which is open to abuse, Paul is careful to instruct about the way those who are at the authority end of those relationships should behave. This is not carte blanche for tyrants. The standards of behaviour are as clear as they are exacting.

But if you are a married woman, you are called upon to submit to your husband out of reverence for Christ.

20

Submission is not as hard as it sounds

Fellow wives, the fact that submission is something you do for Jesus is extremely liberating.

You submit to your husband not because he is Mr Wonderful (though he may be), nor because he is always right (which he won't be). You do not submit to him because he is bigger, stronger, older and cleverer than you, if he should happen to be any of those things. You do it because Jesus asks you to. You do it as to the Lord. That means cheerfully, gladly and with trust. You are under no illusions. Your husband is not Jesus, and you do not worship him as if he were. Jesus has your heart and he is the one you worship. But because you love Jesus you submit to your husband because Jesus knows the best formula for marriage, and this is it.

The words 'in everything' (Ephesians 5:24) might sound daunting. It is of course a comprehensive bracket reminding us that it is not: 'Wives, submit to your husbands—except when you know better.' Or: 'Wife, submit to your husband when you agree with him.'

But for the most part, you won't even realize you are submitting. Mostly your husband will value your input and listen to your point of view, and many decisions will be made mutually and in perfect harmony.

And a wise husband, like our city gate friend from Proverbs 31, will be happy to delegate many decisions to his capable wife. As we said: he has confidence in her. So she is not phoning him up at the office and asking whether she should buy beef or lamb.

It is at the times when you don't agree that submission comes into play. Here is a situation we faced some years ago: we had a growing family and a small house. I thought it was time we moved to something slightly larger and had got details of a house in the area which I thought would accommodate us better. We went to look at it, and I liked it. We talked about it, making our arguments. Ultimately, however, John decided against any move on the grounds of the larger financial commitment it would require. I was disappointed. It was a submission moment. But at that point I dropped the whole thing and never mentioned it again—and guess what? We have been fine in our little house, which we live in to this day.

Somebody had to have the last word in that argument, and I recognized that that person was my husband.

Suppose we had not been fine in our little house. Indeed, there were occasions when it seemed mighty crowded. I might have been tempted to say, 'I told you we should have bought that house …!' But I didn't. By God's grace I realized that this is how it is: John will answer to God for his headship and leadership of this family; I will answer to God for my submission or otherwise.

It really is not that hard. And it is a recipe for a marriage that lasts.

Respect is shown or withheld
sometimes in the smallest
of things which can become
unconscious habits for better
or worse.

3. Submission in practice looks very like respect

At the end of the Ephesians 5 passage on marriage Paul sums up in verse 33:

> However, each one of you also must love his wife as he loves himself, and the wife must respect her husband.

So a different word is used: respect. Respect is submission in everyday clothes. When there is a big decision to be made and you disagree, then submission comes into play. But for the most part you are shuffling along together and the biggest decisions are about the colour you will paint the fence. They are not things to go to war about, and no one need get excited. As a couple you are, as one writer put it, 'sharing the work of survival'. What does submission look like then?

Answer: it looks like respect. That is how you demonstrate on a daily basis in action and attitude that you are not the governor.

Why does Paul not tell wives to love their husbands at this point? This may be going a bit far, but it is possible that Paul tells husbands to love their wives because the besetting sin of the male gender is selfishness. Now, in the case of females, it is not love we are generally lacking. The besetting sin of women is control. Hence the curse of Genesis 3:16: 'Your desire will be for your husband, and he will rule over you.' The desire there is not sexual desire but desire for control; the same word is used in Genesis 4:7, when God describes sin as crouching at the door *desiring* to have the mastery of Cain. So fallen woman loves to control, and thus she must be reminded to respect her husband.

When a woman has no respect for her husband, her marriage is in extreme jeopardy. A man cannot live long in a home where he has no respect. A woman might admit that she no longer loves her husband, but for that marriage there is hope. You can learn to love; if you could not, how is it that the older women of

Titus 2 can train the younger ones to love their husbands? But for the marriage without respect there is less hope because of the critical damage that is daily being inflicted to the God-appointed head of the home.

Respect is shown or withheld sometimes in the smallest of things which can become unconscious habits for better or worse. When you show respect you add supporting nails to the structure of your marriage. When you withhold it you remove them, and one day the whole thing may come clattering down.

> The wise woman builds her house,
>> but with her own hands the foolish one tears hers down (Proverbs 14:1).

So here are some quite everyday ways, some practical ideas, about how to show respect and build the house that is your marriage.

Listen to him

This is respect at its most fundamental. When he is talking, meet his eyes and really listen to what he is saying. He may not be the most articulate of men, but hear him out and resist the temptation to finish his sentences for him. And while you are listening, clear your mind of other things. Sometimes while someone is talking to us, all we are thinking about is our clever reply or our better idea. Women are often quicker with words than men are, and we think we know what they want to say or even what they need. Try listening.

Sometimes I have heard a wife talk about her husband as if he were one of the children—she might even jokingly include him in the number of her children. A sad error. He is not your child and he does not want to be married to his mother. So don't put him down or keep correcting him.

Sometimes a wife complains that her husband doesn't talk to her. And sometimes he is at fault in his unwillingness to share things or let her into his life. But in some cases he has simply given up. Everything he suggested was trumped so he took the easy route. He thinks regarding his wife: since you have the last word, you might as well have the first and all those in between.

When it is him talking, give him your undivided attention.

Give up control

Which includes stopping trying to change him, by the way. Changing your husband is God's work, so don't take that one on.

But a woman's ways of controlling are subtle and devious. She has it down to a fine art. She can manipulate by sulks or by silence; she can just mention things; she can come up with lists or get his friends to gang up on him; she can just go ahead and make plans and decisions and leave him out entirely. Proverbs mentions three times about the pain of living with a nagging wife. Better to live in a desert, says Proverbs 21:19.

One of my favourite love songs of the twentieth century is *She* by Charles Aznavour. In this wonderful tribute to the woman who is undoubtedly the best thing in his life there are some backhanders:

> She may be the beauty or the beast
> May be the famine or the feast
> May turn each day into a heaven or a hell …

Our desire for control can make life hell for a man. I know one young husband who trembles at the Saturday morning list.

For once, why not go with his idea, without making a counter suggestion? Say, 'Yes, that's a great idea! Brilliant!' Don't offer advice unless it's asked for.

Here is an example of my total failure at this one. God graciously enabled me to see what I was doing and I learned a valuable lesson.

We needed to clear out our cellar because we were having it refurbished. Some of the stuff from the cellar had to be relocated to the garden shed. We therefore needed to clear out the garden shed. Now, in the garden shed was a bike, a not very good bike—in fact, a very poor one which no one had used for years. Having 'mentioned' the clearing of the shed on a number of occasions I lost patience one day and started some clearing on my own. I removed the bike from the shed, put it by the back door, and when my husband came home for lunch (in the middle of a busy day) suggested that on his way back to work he could drop the bike off at the local school, because they were due to have a sale the following Saturday.

I could not understand why my husband stared at me in disbelief. But sober reflection opened my eyes to the fact that I had completely excluded him from a number of stages in this process:

- I had taken on the task of clearing the shed despite having asked him to do it.

- We had never discussed the bike and what we would do with it.

- I had assumed I knew what his plans were for the afternoon.

In other words, I had in my subtle way been totally disrespectful. I learned and resolved that I would not mention about clearing cellar or shed again. And sure enough, the day came when he got up and expressed his intention to set about the shed. Win, win. I could smile and be delighted and encouraging; he cheerfully got stuck in and followed through on his own plan. And both cellar and shed got cleared.

It is so much better to give up control.

Even when you express your desires, resist the temptation to tell him when, where and how.

Be captivating
One way of showing respect is to make an effort to look nice for him. This is going to sound terribly twee but I must tell you about my mother who was a classic 1950s housewife. An abiding memory of my childhood is that at about 5.30 on every weekday afternoon she would go upstairs to her bedroom, change her dress, apply lipstick and powder, and generally spruce up so that, as she told me at the time, she would be a nice sight for my father when he came in the door. Call it old-fashioned, but isn't there something wonderful about it? Wouldn't that make a man feel welcomed in his own home?

If you are based at home, what greets your husband when he walks through the door? Chaos and bad temper? A cursory nod and carry on texting? As the song says, 'Little things mean a lot.'

In the warning against adultery in Proverbs 5, the writer paints a delightful picture of lasting married happiness:

> May your fountain be blessed
>   and may you rejoice in the wife of your youth.
> A loving doe, a graceful deer—
>   may her breasts satisfy you always,
>   may you ever be captivated by her love (Proverbs 5:18–19).

So the message is, fellow wives, be captivating. Don't let yourself go. Don't slob around in a T-shirt and joggers unless you really are doing something which requires manky old clothes. Wear the kinds of clothes to make him smile. If those are not the kind you can wear to church, so be it. Collect a set for his eyes only. Charity shops can be a good cheap source of captivating clothes.

The message this kind of thing gives is that your husband is important in your world. Be an endearing companion for him, one he will be proud to take out. Kiss him enthusiastically. Say yes to sex. Or if you say no, say when.

God doesn't do dowdy. And a lasting marriage doesn't do dowdy either.

Empower right behaviour

It's not just the outside. Of course not. In 1 Peter 3 we are reminded of the priority of the inside, the beauty of the gentle and quiet spirit. Peter says these kinds of winning ways might even win an unbelieving husband for Christ. Without words. And if it can do good in that kind of home, how much more where both parties are Christian! The purity and reverence of life that Peter talks about has to be fuelled by time spent in prayer and in godly priorities. Those women had apostolic teaching to shape their lives. We have the whole Scripture to help us set godly priorities. Such things have an impact for good, so time spent in prayer and Bible reading is never wasted.

Suppose, for example, you are a wife with a Christian husband, but you feel that family prayers have truly been neglected in your home. You feel strongly about this, strong enough to mention it. It is OK to ask, even to persuade. But gently and not overmuch. You might, like Abigail (1 Samuel 25), be an effective persuader. Her style of argument is an interesting study. But if not, then you pray.

Is your husband important enough that you pray for him every day?

Support his work

Have respect for the work he does, whether it is what he does for money to provide for the family or what he does for love by serving in the church.

Many men do really stressful or boring jobs and endure horrible commutes for years and years just because they want to support their families. If that is the case, make sure your husband knows how much you appreciate the sacrifice he is making.

You may be in salaried employment yourself. If so, you will have your own battles to face and pressures to manage. I am not denying those. As I have said, there has to be a sharing in the work of survival. But respect for your husband will mean that you are never in competition with him, that you show interest and support in what he does, as you would hope he would do for you.

Perhaps you have a husband who is very active in church life. It is splendid to engage in serving the Lord side by side: you can then demonstrate so clearly what your marriage is about. But perhaps his service for God will mean that he is out several nights a week while you are in with the children. Look on the sacrifice you make as something you can do for the Lord, releasing your husband and his gifts to kingdom work. Don't complain or argue when he returns. Be glad that he has a heart which loves God best.

Admire him and receive gladly his strength and leadership

Don't be one of those touchy feminists who snarl at a man for opening a door. Encourage and show pleasure and gratitude for any expressions of manliness.

It is really hard to be a man, in the biblical sense of the word, in the days in which we live. It is even harder to be a Christian man. Your husband may not express it, but he will frequently be suffering extreme insecurity. He will benefit from your telling him when he has done well.

Admire him physically. The Song of Songs may sound a bit bizarre with its mentions of chrysolite and polished ivory, but what is clear is that verbal expression of delight in each other is extremely biblical. Not just your words, but also your smile and your touch will be his mirror to help him through the crises of life or just the times when everything seems to conspire to beat him down.

And when he admires you, receive the compliment graciously. Don't deny it and go on about the size of your bottom. He probably likes it like that anyway.

Let him do things for you too. I remember being extremely cross when I saw John brushing the stairs. I felt he was making a comment on my standard of domesticity, which was pretty low. But really he was just serving and helping, recognizing that as a mother of four young children, my hands were pretty full and dust was accumulating. I should have thanked him for his consideration and support instead of being defensive and grouchy.

Let him be a father to his children, and not another mother. Mothers and fathers are not interchangeable, whatever people today might say. God meant it like that, so be glad. So if he fizzes the children up playing wild games before bedtime, be glad for his involvement. If he dresses them totally inappropriately, just go with it. He's a man. He doesn't have your categories for matching outfits and winter- and summer-weight clothing. But he does love his children and delight in them. That's a father.

It is great to have a man in the house.

Conclusion:
Don't wear a crown, be one

Your submission enables your husband to gladly be what God wants him to be. It is very difficult to lead in a home where everything you do is criticized. Some women have said to me, 'I wish my husband would lead. But if I didn't take action, nothing would get done.' Frequently what has happened in that marriage is that the man has run for cover. He is afraid of his wife's disapproval and fails to take initiative.

In the days when everyone wore hats, there used to be an advertisement on the London Underground that said, 'If you want to get ahead, wear a hat.' The Bible says to married women, 'If you want to have a head, be a crown.'

> A wife of noble character is her husband's crown,
> but a disgraceful wife is like decay in his bones (Proverbs 12:4).

So there it is. You can be a crown or a cancer. You can debilitate him, or you can make him look good, proud to hold his head up, an effective and happy leader in his family.

That is what God wants him to be. And that is what most women want too: a man they can really look up to.

Trust God and take his path, the path of submission. It is the way to a God-honouring marriage, which as a matter of fact will also be a happier one.

And this is a marriage that will last.